Cambridge English Readers

Level 2

Series editor: Philip Prowse

The Double Bass Mystery

Jeremy Harmer

PUBLISHED BY THE PRESS SYNDICATE OF THE UNIVERSITY OF CAMBRIDGE
The Pitt Building, Trumpington Street, Cambridge CB2 1RP, United Kingdom

CAMBRIDGE UNIVERSITY PRESS
The Edinburgh Building, Cambridge CB2 2RU, United Kingdom
40 West 20th Street, New York, NY 10011-4211, USA
10 Stamford Road, Oakleigh, Melbourne 3166, Australia

First published 1999
Reprinted 1999

Printed in the United Kingdom at J.W. Arrowsmith Ltd, Bristol
Typeset in 12/15pt Adobe Garamond [CE]
Illustrations by Sam Thompson

ISBN 0 521 65613 3

Contents

People in the story

Marilyn Whittle –
Harp

Frank Shepherd –
Orchestra Manager

Adriana Fox –
Violin

Martin Audley –
Trumpet

Philip Worth –
Conductor

Penny Wade –
Double Bass

Simon Hunt –
Double Bass

Candida Ashley-Morton –
Double Bass

Inspector Jorge Portillo

Chapter 1 *A bit of a problem*

We came out of the airport building. All eighty-five players from the Barston Symphony Orchestra in England. The sun was shining. It was hot.

'Welcome to Barcelona!' Frank Shepherd said to us all. 'Come this way. The coaches are waiting.' We followed him. Somebody took a photograph.

The coaches left the airport and started on the motorway into Barcelona. Frank Shepherd came and sat next to me. Frank is the manager of the Barston Symphony Orchestra.

'Penny,' he said (that's my name). 'We've got a bit of a problem.'

'What kind of a problem?' I said.

'Well, it's your double bass,' he said.

'My double bass? What's wrong with my double bass?'

'It isn't here. It isn't in Barcelona.'

'What? Where is it?'

'I'm afraid that I just don't know,' Frank said.

Oh, sorry. I must tell you something about me because, well, this is my story. Actually that's not quite true. It's the story of a double bass too. People take things and somebody dies. But that's for later. Now I'll start at the beginning.

My name is Penny Wade. I am twenty-six years old. I play the double bass in the Barston Symphony Orchestra. There are eight double basses in the BSO. I am number eight. I got the job six months ago. The other seven players are all older or better than me. The trip to Spain was my first time with the orchestra in a foreign country.

'What's the problem?' my friend Adriana said from the seat behind me. Adriana plays the violin in the orchestra.

'It's my double bass,' I said. 'Frank can't find it.'

'I'm sorry,' Frank said. 'We put it in the BSO truck in Barston and it wasn't in the truck when it arrived in Barcelona.'

All the big instruments came by road. It was cheaper than taking them in a plane.

'He says someone's taken it,' I told Adriana.

'I said *perhaps* someone's taken it,' Frank said.

'That's no help at all,' I said. I was angry. '*Perhaps* isn't any good. Perhaps it fell off the truck. Perhaps someone wanted wood for their fire . . .'

'Look,' Adriana said. 'This is stupid. Double basses are big. They don't just fall off trucks.'

'This one did,' I said. I looked out of the window of the coach. We were arriving in Barcelona. My first foreign trip. Wonderful, don't you think? But that's just the problem. It wasn't wonderful at all.

Chapter 2 *A beautiful day*

I woke up. I looked around me. Where was I? Then I remembered. I was in a hotel in Barcelona. With the Barston Symphony Orchestra. But without my double bass.

I went to the dining room and had coffee. Simon Hunt was at my table. I was his girlfriend, and he was my boyfriend. I think.

'Listen,' he said. 'You know tonight's concert.'

'Yes,' I said, 'and I can't play in it.'

'Well, you can if you want,' he smiled. 'You can play in my place.'

'Oh Simon, really?'

'Yes, I've hurt my hand, so … erm … I can't play, you see.'

I looked at his hand. I couldn't see anything wrong.

'It looks OK,' I said.

'Well, it isn't,' he answered quickly.

I liked Simon very much. He was tall and handsome. He had dark hair and blue eyes. He was double bass number two in our orchestra and ten years older than me.

'Are you all right?' I put my hand on his arm.

'I'll be fine.' He took my hand away. 'I've talked to Candida about tonight.' (Candida was the leader of the double basses.) 'She says it's OK.'

'Thanks, Simon.'

'Yes, well, it's nothing. It means that I get a free afternoon.'

'Well, we're both free this morning,' I said. 'We can do something together.'

'Hmmm,' he said.

'Perhaps we can go to the Picasso museum. Or the Parc Güell? Or up to Montjuïc? Or to the beach?' (Barcelona's got everything: beautiful buildings, good restaurants, the sea.)

'Yes,' said Simon. He wasn't listening to me at all.

'You're not listening to me at all!' I said.

'Sorry?' he said, looking back at me.

'I said "You're not listening to me at all".'

'OK, OK, sorry. It's just, well, I've got a lot that I have to think about.' He looked strange.

'Do you want to do something together this morning or not?' I asked.

'No. No, I don't ...'

At that moment Adriana walked over to our table. 'Morning!' she said happily. 'It's a beautiful day. What are you two going to do today?'

'I don't know,' I said. I was watching Simon. He was smiling at Adriana.

'Well, look,' she said to me. 'We've got lots of free time. Let's go to the beach or something.'

'Yes, that's a great idea.' I was pleased. It was going to be a good day after all, I thought. But I didn't know what was going to happen then, did I?

Chapter 3 *A newspaper, a beach*

While I was waiting for Adriana in the hotel reception area I sat down at a table. There were newspapers on the table. Most of them were in Spanish or Catalan, but there was one from Britain. I began to read it. There was a story about a painting.

Thieves Steal Picture from Gallery

The Gardener

Two nights ago some men got into the Tate Gallery in London. They took a painting called *The Gardener* by the French painter Cézanne.

'It's one of our most famous pictures,' said gallery director Delia Hitchin. 'Everyone loves it. *The Gardener* is a beautiful picture. It is a good example of Cézanne's work.'

The thieves got in through a window at the back of the building. Nobody heard them. Nobody saw them. They cut the painting from its frame.

'This painting is really important,' says Ms Hitchin. 'We want it back. Please, if you know anything at all call us or the police.'

The Gardener is 65.4 x 54 centimetres. It is worth about two million pounds.

I looked up. Frank Shepherd was standing next to my chair. He was looking at the newspaper too.

'That's an interesting story,' he said.

'What story?'

'About the painting.'

'The thieves were very good,' I said. 'Nobody saw them in the gallery. Nobody heard them.'

'Yes. That's good all right,' Frank said. 'Oh, by the way, about your double bass.'

'Yes?' I said.

'I talked to the police here. A man called Portillo.'

'And?' I asked.

'He's going to try and find it,' Frank said.

'How?' I said. I wanted my double bass back.

'I don't know. I'm not a policeman. He's going to talk to the drivers of the truck, I think. And he's going to talk to the French police.'

At that moment we heard a voice.

'Frank!' somebody shouted. 'Frank Shepherd! I want to talk to you.'

I looked round. Candida Ashley-Morton, the leader of the double basses, was walking towards us.

'Excuse me!' said Frank. He walked up to Candida and the two of them went towards the hotel bar. Candida was talking quickly. Was she angry? I couldn't hear the conversation. They went into the bar.

The lift doors opened and Adriana got out with some of the other orchestra players.

Somebody was shouting in the hotel bar. It was Candida Ashley-Morton. She was shouting at Frank. There was a

11

short silence. Then he shouted back. Everybody stood and listened.

'Come on,' Adriana said to us. 'It's their problem, not ours. Let's go to the beach and have some fun!'

If you haven't been to Barcelona, you must go. The city feels good and there's lots to do. One of the most famous areas of the city is a big street called *Les Rambles* – or the Ramblas in English. People walk in the middle of this street. Cars go on the sides. Tourists walk up and down it. It has trees and cafés, street musicians and street actors. People sell newspapers and flowers and birds in cages. They try and sell you things or paint your picture. It's always full of life, always full of people.

About twenty of us left the hotel that morning. We walked down the Ramblas. We were talking and laughing. At the bottom of the long street we walked past the boats and the restaurants and then we came to the beach.

It was a beautiful day. The sun was already high in the sky. There were a lot of people lying on the sand. Some of the orchestra ran to the sea and swam. Some began to play football on the beach. Adriana and I sat and watched. We put on our sunglasses and smiled at each other.

'Wow!' she said. 'This is fantastic! This is the life!'

She was right. It was a fantastic day. But we didn't know, then, about the future. The future wasn't fantastic at all.

Chapter 4   *The concert*

Concerts start late in Spain. It was half past nine and the theatre still wasn't full. My face was red because of the day's sun and it was very hot in the theatre.

At five to ten we walked on to the theatre stage and sat down. The audience stopped talking. Our conductor, Philip Worth, walked on to the stage at ten o'clock. He lifted his arms and we started to play a piece of music called 'In the South' by the English composer Edward Elgar. I looked at all the people in the audience. Simon was near the front. He smiled at me. I was playing very well. I was really happy – except for Simon's poor hand, of course.

After 'In the South' we played a guitar concerto by the Spanish composer Rodrigo. The guitarist was a young Catalan player. She was very good and everybody loved her. Then there was a break of twenty minutes before the second half of the concert. The orchestra went into a room behind the stage. We drank some water. Simon came in.

'That was great,' he said. 'You're playing very well.'

'Thanks,' I said. I was very happy. 'It's because of your instrument. It's because of you.'

'Don't say that,' he laughed.

'Why?' I asked him.

'It's not true.' For a minute he didn't look happy.

'Sorry,' I said.

He smiled at me. 'I'm going to sit at the back of the theatre for the second half,' he told me. 'OK?'

'Why?' I asked.

'To hear a different sound,' he answered. 'To hear you from the back of the theatre.'

'Oh, right. I understand.' Except I didn't really understand. Then he kissed my hand and I felt happy. Simon wasn't always nice to me.

'See you later,' I said.

We played Rachmaninov's Third Symphony after the break. It is difficult music, but I think we played it well. The audience were very happy, anyway.

I left the stage with Simon's double bass. I put it into its big white case and closed it. Then I looked for Simon, but he wasn't in the theatre. I went to the room behind the stage. Many of the orchestra players were there. They were talking happily. I waited for Simon. But he didn't come.

'Have you seen Simon?' I asked Adriana.

'Me? No. Why?' She was a bit red in the face. I told you. It was a very hot night.

'I can't find him,' I said, looking at her. 'He was at the front of the theatre for the first half. Then he went to the back. Now he isn't there.'

'He's probably at the hotel.'

'I hope so,' I told her.

'And another thing,' she said. 'Where's Frank?'

'Isn't he here?' I asked.

'I don't think so,' she said. 'I can't see him, anyway.'

I left the theatre with her. We talked about the concert. She said that everybody loved it. Yes, I agreed, it was really good.

We walked along the Ramblas. There were people out with their friends. Men and women. Boyfriends and girlfriends. Children. It was a lovely night. There was a man with a guitar. A woman was dancing to his music. People sat in the open-air cafés and drank beer and wine.

'It's a bit late for children,' I said.

'Not here,' Adriana said. This was her third time in Barcelona. 'Here everybody goes to bed very late.'

'Well, I can't understand it,' I answered. 'I'm very tired. I want to go to sleep.'

Ten minutes later we got to our hotel.

I didn't say goodnight to Simon. I couldn't find him.

'Do you want a drink?' Adriana asked.

'No thanks. I really am very tired.'

'OK,' she said, 'see you tomorrow morning.'

I got into the lift and went up to my floor. I thought about the concert. I thought I played well.

When I got to my room I went to the telephone. I tried

a number. No answer. I put the telephone down. I thought something was wrong. I wasn't happy. Simon wasn't with me. My lovely double bass wasn't with me.

'Oh well,' I thought. 'Maybe tomorrow will be better.'

Some people think the double bass is a funny instrument. They say it just goes *plonk plonk*, but it's not true. Double basses are wonderful. They look lovely and they have a warm sound – like a friend. They are different from other instruments, too. I mean, one violin looks a lot like another violin. Cellos all look the same too. (Well, maybe they're different colours, but most people think they look the same.) So do trumpets. But not double basses. Some are tall and thin, some are short and fat. Each one is a different person. Each one has its own sound.

My double bass is a dark rich brown. It's very old. It looks really beautiful. If you play it well it makes a special sound. And it is worth a lot of money. I love it more than anything else. It's a Panormo. Made in 1798. My parents bought it for me.

'What am I going to do without my beautiful Panormo?' I thought. 'And where is Simon? What is happening to me?'

I was very tired. I fell asleep.

Chapter 5 *Screams in the night*

I was asleep, but my head was full of pictures and stories. I was dreaming about double basses and violinists and parties on the beach. Simon was in my dream. Our conductor was in it. So was my old teacher, playing a double bass on the sand. Then I heard a different sound. Somebody was shouting. No, it was worse than that. Somebody was screaming, screaming very loudly. I opened my eyes. I woke up. It was five o'clock in the morning.

Somebody screamed again. And again. And again. This time I wasn't dreaming.

I got out of bed. I put on a T-shirt and some jeans and went out of my room. Doors were opening on the left and the right. Adriana came out of her room. She ran up to me. She was half asleep, still in her night-dress. 'What is it?' she asked sleepily. 'What's going on?'

'I don't know,' I answered.

Martin Audley (a trumpet player) came up to us.

'Who screamed?' he asked.

'Nobody knows,' I told him. 'But it sounded terrible.'

There was another scream. It came from outside.

We ran back into my room and looked out of the window, down at the street. There was a police car there, some people, more and more people. And something else.

'Come on,' I said. We got the lift to the ground floor. When it stopped we ran out of the hotel and pushed to the front of all the people.

Marilyn Whittle, the harp player, was already there. Her face was white and her eyes were large and round.

'Look! Look!' she said. She was pointing in front of her. She screamed again.

We looked. She was pointing at the person at her feet. It was Frank Shepherd. His mouth was open. There was blood all over his head.

Martin spoke first. 'My God!' he said. 'He's dead!'

For a few minutes nobody did anything. It was like a moment from a bad film. I looked around me. Candida Ashley-Morton was there. Her face was white.

'Oh, oh, oh no,' she was saying, and then she turned and walked back into the hotel.

We knew that we couldn't sleep. We didn't know what to do. But the hotel manager was a nice person. He opened the bar – at half past five in the morning. We sat there. We were all asking the same questions. What happened? How did Frank die? Did he fall from his room?

We heard another police car. A man came into the bar. We stopped talking.

'Good morning,' he said. 'My name is Portillo, Inspector Portillo.' His voice was cold. So were his eyes. But I also thought, 'He's very good-looking with his dark hair and those eyes'. Then I felt bad because of Frank.

'Now, please listen everybody,' the policeman said. 'Mr Shepherd is dead. We can't change that. So go to bed. We'll talk tomorrow – well, I mean later today.' His English was very good.

Outside it was getting light. I was lying on my bed, thinking about Frank. I was trying not to see the blood and his eyes, open and dead. I was trying not to, but I couldn't stop. Someone knocked on my door. I got up and opened it. It was Simon.

'Hello,' he said.

'Hi. Isn't it terrible?'

'Yes,' he said. 'Poor Frank.'

'Where were you?' I asked. 'After the concert? Where were you last night?'

'I went to a bar,' he said.

'Why?' I asked.

'Why? Why? What a stupid question. For a drink.'

'What did you do then?' I asked.

'Questions, questions! Why all these questions?' His voice was different now.

'What did you do then?' I asked again.

'I went to another bar.' He wasn't smiling now.

'Why didn't you tell me?' I said. 'I needed you.' I was thinking of Frank's body again. 'You didn't come to my room when you got back.'

'Is that a question or a statement?'

'I don't know. Come on, Simon, where were you?' I didn't want to ask all these questions but I couldn't help it.

'All right. All right,' he shouted. 'Look, I went to a few bars, OK? I had a lot to drink. A lot. I walked back to the hotel very late. About three in the morning. When I got here I went up to my room quickly. I wasn't feeling very well, you see. All those drinks . . . '

'Were you with someone else?'

'Haven't you listened to me?' Now he was really angry. I didn't understand it.

'Oh Simon, I'm sorry,' I said. 'I'm being stupid. It's just, well, you know . . . '

'Yes,' he said. He was quieter now. 'It's been a difficult night, a difficult morning.' He smiled at me. He kissed me. But there was something wrong. Something wasn't quite right.

'I'm going to go back to my room,' he said. 'I need a shower. See you later.' He walked out of the room without another word.

I looked at the closed door. I thought about his words, about his answers to my questions. And then I thought, 'Why isn't he telling me the truth?'

Chapter 6 *Inspector Portillo*

Three and a half hours later on that same day I sat down with Inspector Portillo in the hotel dining room.

'Good morning, Miss Wade,' he said.

'Good morning,' I answered. I was a bit afraid. Why did he want to see me? Why were the police talking to everybody?

'I know about you,' he said.

'You do?' I asked.

'Yes. You're the player with the double bass.'

'Without the double bass,' I said.

'Yes,' he laughed. 'But we're looking for it.'

'Will you find it?' I asked.

'I hope so.'

'He isn't cold,' I thought. 'He's very nice. I like him.'

Then, suddenly, he changed. 'Now I have some questions for you.'

'Why?' I asked.

'That is not a very intelligent question,' he said. 'Someone has died. We always ask questions.'

'So you think I'm stupid, do you?' I was angry and very, very tired.

'No, of course not. I am very sorry,' he said. I looked into his face. He really *was* sorry.

'Forget it!' I said. 'I'm just tired.'

'Yes, so am I,' he smiled. 'Now, can I ask you some questions?'

'Yes,' I answered unhappily.

'Where were you last night?' he said suddenly.

'I was at the concert,' I replied.

'Yes, yes. Of course. And after the concert?'

'I came back to the hotel.'

'Who with?' said Inspector Portillo.

'With Adriana Fox. We walked up the Ramblas together.'

'OK,' Portillo said. 'You got back to the hotel. And then?'

'And then I went to bed,' I explained.

'Just you?' he asked with a smile.

'What? What do you mean?' I said.

'Are you married?' he asked. 'Do you have a boyfriend?'

'I'm not married. But I've got a boyfriend,' I said. 'I think.'

'Who is he?' Inspector Portillo asked.

'Do you have to know?' I asked. 'Is it important?'

'I'll ask you a different question,' he said. His voice was cold again. I didn't understand why. 'Do you have a boyfriend in the orchestra?'

'That's a very personal question,' I said.

'Death is very personal,' he said, very quietly.

'Yes. Sorry,' I said. I suddenly saw Frank's body again.

'So?' he asked.

'What?' I said.

'What's the answer? Do you have a boyfriend in the orchestra?'

'Yes,' I said.

'Who is that?'

'Simon Hunt,' I told him.

'And did he, did you spend the night together?'

'Well no, we didn't,' I said. I wasn't enjoying this.

'I see.' He put his pen in his mouth. He didn't say anything for a moment. Then he looked into my eyes. 'All right,' he said. 'That's all.'

'You aren't going to ask me any more questions?' I said, 'I can go?'

'Yes. For now. But don't go far. Nobody in the orchestra must leave Barcelona. Stay near the hotel.'

'Of course.'

'I'll talk to you again,' he said. He was smiling again. 'All right?'

'Oh yes,' I said. 'Good.' But I didn't feel good at all.

Chapter 7   *Secrets*

'It's going to be strange without Frank,' Adriana said.

'Yes,' I agreed. 'Very strange.'

We were sitting in a café. Adriana was drinking an orange juice and I was drinking my third cup of coffee. We both felt very sad.

'You've been in the orchestra for two months,' Adriana said. 'I've been in it for three years. Frank was like a father to me. He was a nice man.'

'Yes,' I said. We talked about Frank. We didn't talk about his body in the street, but I remembered everything. I remembered the screams. I remembered the people in the street, people running in the hotel, Martin, Candida, Adriana. Pictures, pictures. In my head. I sat up. Some coffee fell on to my T-shirt. Something in the pictures was wrong.

'Are you OK?' Adriana asked.

'Yes. No.' I needed time to think. I didn't want questions from Adriana.

'Listen, Penny . . .' she began.

'Yes?' I said.

'Oh, nothing,' she replied. Then she looked up at someone behind me. I turned round.

'Simon!' I said. 'Hello. Where have you been?'

'Oh, here and there,' he replied. 'I was talking to some of the orchestra players. About Frank, of course.'

'Of course,' I said. 'Do you want to sit down?'

'Sure.' Adriana smiled at him. He smiled back. It was a special smile. They had a secret. Just the two of them. Something that I did not know. That nobody knew. I turned away.

Simon asked for a beer. When it came he drank it very quickly.

'What do you think's going to happen?' Adriana asked.

'About what?' Simon said.

'About our concerts – tomorrow here in Barcelona, then Madrid, Bilbao,' Adriana said.

'What do you mean?' Simon asked.

'Well,' my friend explained. 'Frank's dead. He was our orchestra manager. He's been with the orchestra for twenty years. How can we play tomorrow night without him?'

'But it's an important concert tomorrow night,' I said. 'More than two thousand people are coming.'

'Yes, that's a problem,' said a voice next to me. I looked up. Martin Audley was standing there.

'Martin,' said Adriana. She looked uncomfortable. 'What are you doing here?'

'I'm looking for Penny, actually,' Martin told her.

'Me?' I said.

'Yes,' Martin said. 'Inspector Portillo wants to speak to you again.'

'When?' I asked.

'Now. This minute.'

'I'll go then.' I looked at Simon. He wasn't smiling at all now.

I got up and walked away from the table. I looked back. Martin was sitting with them now. The sun was hot but I began to run. I was running away from the picture in my head. The picture of last night in the hotel.

But I couldn't stop the picture. I was back in the hotel, back in my room. I heard the screams. I ran out of my room. Other people ran out of their rooms. Other players.

Adriana, for example. Her room was six doors down from mine. I could see her, but now I remembered something else. She came from her room, but she wasn't the only one there. Somebody was in the room with her. I saw him in the dark, but I couldn't see him well. Who was it?

I thought of Adriana in the café. Smiling at Simon. Was that their secret?

I ran into the hotel. Inspector Portillo was waiting for me.

'I am very sorry,' he started. 'But I have got some more questions.'

'So have I,' I said. 'Did somebody kill Frank?'

'Maybe.' He smiled a secret smile.

'What do you mean by "maybe"? Have you found Frank's killer? What do you know?' I asked.

'Miss Wade,' he said. 'There's something the police here always do, something we have always done.'

'What's that?' I asked, stupidly.

'Well, *we* ask the questions, *you* give the answers.' I think he was laughing at me. 'Is that all right with you?' he asked.

I didn't say anything.

'That means yes, I think. Now Mr Simon Hunt is your boyfriend, you said?' asked the inspector.

'Yes,' I answered.

'And he plays the double bass too, I believe?'

'Yes,' I said.

'Is he a good bass player?'

'Oh yes,' I said immediately. 'He's better than me. He's the number two. The second best in the whole orchestra.'

'Yes,' the inspector said. 'Somebody told me that.'

'Why are we talking about Simon?' I asked, but he didn't answer me. He just looked and looked. 'Sorry,' I said, 'I remember. *You* ask the questions.'

'You are a quick learner Miss Wade.' Now I was sure. He was laughing at me. 'Mr Hunt didn't play in the concert last night, did he?' he said suddenly.

'No,' I told him. 'I played in his place. He lent me his double bass. Because I haven't got mine with me.'

'Yes,' he said. 'I haven't forgotten.'

'Sorry, of course not,' I said. Was he angry with me?

'Did Simon Hunt go to the concert?' he asked.

'Oh yes. He was at the front,' I told him. I was thinking of Simon's handsome face.

'Was he at the front all the time?' Inspector Portillo said.

'No. In the second half he sat at the back.'

'Did you see him at the back?' His voice was cold again.

'Yes. I mean, no.' I wasn't sure. 'It's a big theatre.'

'And after the concert?' the inspector asked. 'What did Mr Hunt do then?'

'He went to a bar – well, he went to three or four bars I think,' I told him.

'Did you see him at the hotel?'

'No . . . look, why are you asking all these questions about Simon? You should ask me about Candida,' I said.

'Candida?' he said.

'Yes, Candida Ashley-Morton,' I said. 'The leader of the double basses.'

'What about her?'

'I think . . . I think that perhaps she killed Frank,' I said. 'Well, perhaps she didn't kill him, but she knows something. I'm sure.'

'Why do you say that?' he asked.

'Well, because I heard something. She was very angry with him yesterday morning.' I told Inspector Portillo about the conversation between Candida and Frank in the hotel bar.

When I finished he sat back in his chair.

'That is most interesting, Miss Wade,' he said. 'Most interesting.'

'Well, yes. So you must talk to them.'

'Thank you,' said the police inspector. 'I will think about it. And Penny – I mean, Miss Wade – I am sorry about all the questions.'

I got up and walked out of the room. Candida Ashley-Morton. Yes. Perhaps she killed Frank. Did the inspector believe that? Did I? What was the truth?

Twenty-four hours later I had the answer.

Chapter 8   *A restaurant, a fight*

That evening some of us went to a restaurant near the Ramblas. Simon didn't come with us.

'I have to see some people. I'll come back to the hotel later,' he told me. I was sitting next to Martin. I like Martin. He's been in the orchestra for about six years.

Adriana was at the other side of the table. Sometimes she smiled at me and I smiled back. But all the time I was thinking, 'Was that Simon in her room? Is she trying to be my friend and Simon's lover at the same time?' He wasn't in his room last night. Somebody was in hers.

'Oh no,' I thought. 'Why is life so difficult?'

We finished our supper and paid the bill. Then we walked back up the Ramblas.

Adriana came up to me. 'Are you OK?' she said. We were walking past a café.

'Now, now,' I thought. 'Now is a good time for the question – the question I want to ask her.'

But at that moment we heard English voices. We turned round. Candida Ashley-Morton was sitting at one of the tables. Marilyn Whittle, the harp player, was standing up. She was shouting at Candida. People were watching them.

'Was it you?' she was shouting. 'Did you push him out of the window?'

'No, of course, I didn't,' Candida said quietly. 'Don't be stupid.'

'I think you did,' the harp player said. 'You killed him. Because he didn't love you.'

'What are you talking about?' Candida's face was white.

'You loved him, didn't you?' Marilyn said. Her face was all red.

Candida looked at the ground. She didn't say anything.

'Didn't you?' screamed Marilyn. 'You were in love with him!'

'All right. It's true,' Candida said. 'Frank and I were lovers. There, are you happy?'

'That's why you killed him!' Marilyn shouted.

'What are you talking about?' Candida said again. Her voice sounded tired.

'You killed him because he didn't love you anymore,' Marilyn told her.

'Please stop. Everyone's listening.'

'Everybody's listening?' she said. 'So what? Let them listen. I'll tell them a story. About a man called Frank Shepherd. I loved him too, you know.'

'Yes,' Candida said quietly. 'He told me.'

'That's not true!' the harp player shouted back. 'He didn't tell you. He didn't love you. He loved me. More than you. He loved me.'

'Stop it, Marilyn,' Candida said. 'Go back to the hotel. Go back to your room. You need some sleep.'

'Sleep? I can't sleep. Frank's dead. How can I sleep? With a killer in the next room.'

'Now listen, Marilyn, you must stop this.'

'I won't stop it. You're a killer, a killer, a dirty killer. You pushed him out of that window because he loved me.

Me. He loved me.' Marilyn was shouting louder and louder. She had a terrible look in her eyes. Everybody on the street stopped to watch. I didn't know what to do.

Adriana walked over to the harp player. 'Stop it!' she said to her. 'Stop it!' And she hit Marilyn hard in the face.

Marilyn opened her mouth to say something. Then she closed it and ran out of the café.

'Go after her, Martin,' Adriana said, and Martin followed the unhappy harp player into the night.

'I'm sorry about that,' Candida said, 'I'm sorry. It's not true, of course. Really. It's not true.' She was crying now.

'Let's talk about it tomorrow,' Adriana said. She put her arm around Candida and we walked away, up the Ramblas, towards our hotel.

I spent that night with Simon. He arrived an hour after we did. He was nice to me. He got into bed next to me, and kissed my eyes. He talked of love and I wanted to believe him. He had a bottle of champagne with him.

But I wasn't happy. I loved Simon, but I didn't feel good about it. He was strange towards me. Sometimes he said things and did things which I didn't understand. But he tried to love me, I think. He tried to love me that night, perhaps because he knew something that I didn't know. He knew that it was our last night together.

When I woke up he was gone.

Chapter 9 *Two men, a truck, and a double bass*

I couldn't find Simon after breakfast. I couldn't find him anywhere in the hotel.

The morning passed very slowly. The orchestra players talked to each other, but not much. A few of us went for a walk, but we didn't go far. We were all waiting.

After lunch we all went back to the hotel dining room. Well, nearly all of us.

Philip Worth, our conductor, walked into the room. Inspector Portillo was with him.

'Good afternoon, everybody,' said our conductor. Everybody stopped talking.

'Now as you know, Inspector Portillo asked you all questions yesterday. Now he has some answers. Jorge.'

Jorge? Inspector Jorge Portillo. That was the inspector's name? I liked it.

'Thank you, *Maestro*,' said Inspector Portillo. 'At this moment we don't know everything. We have to talk to some more people. But I will tell you my idea of the story. I think it is the real story, but . . . ' he looked around the room, 'some things are still not clear.' He looked at me and smiled.

'You all came to Barcelona by air,' he started. 'Because it's quicker than a coach. But the big instruments came in the BSO truck with two drivers. The double basses were in that truck, of course. They drove to Dover and put the truck on the boat. Then they drove through France towards Spain.

After twelve hours the truck drivers were tired. They stopped at a café by the side of the road. Near Toulouse in France. They went into the café and had a cup of coffee and something to eat. Then a car arrived. A big car, I think. It went up to the truck. Two men got out – well, we think it was two. They went to the truck. They opened it – I'm sure they had the key. Then they saw *it* and they smiled.'

'What? What did they see?' Marilyn asked.

'The double bass of Miss Penny Wade,' said the inspector.

'What? What did they see?' I asked.

'They saw your double bass, Miss Wade.'

'Why my double bass?' I didn't understand what he was talking about. 'They weren't looking for it, were they?'

'Oh yes,' Inspector Portillo said. 'That's what they were looking for.'

'But who? Why? How did they know it was my double bass?' I asked.

'I think somebody wrote your name on the case. The two men saw it and they took it from the truck.'

'I don't understand,' Adriana said. 'Why did they take Penny's double bass?'

'Well, I don't think they wanted Miss Wade's instrument,' the inspector said. 'They wanted the case.'

'The case?' Martin said. 'Why did they want the case?'

'Well, actually,' Inspector Portillo said. 'They didn't want the case. They wanted something in the case.'

'What? What was it?' I couldn't wait any longer.

'A picture.'

'A picture? What kind of a picture?' Adriana asked.

'It was a painting. By the French artist Cézanne. It's called "The Gardener". Somebody took it from the Tate Gallery in London ...'

'Oh yes,' I shouted. 'I read about it in the paper. It's worth two million pounds. Wow!'

'Thank you Miss Wade,' said Inspector Portillo. I wasn't sure, but I think he was smiling at me again. I smiled back. 'So somebody took the painting from the Tate Gallery. And then somebody – it wasn't the same person, of course – put it in Miss Wade's double bass case.'

'Why didn't they take the picture and leave the double bass?' I asked.

'I don't know. Perhaps they didn't have time. Perhaps some people came out of the café. But they closed the truck and drove away with Miss Wade's bass in its big white case.'

'Inspector,' Martin said. 'You say "I think", "perhaps", "I don't know". What do you *know*? Is this story true?'

'That's a good question,' Inspector Portillo replied.

'Yes, but what's the answer?' Martin said.

'The answer is this. Miss Wade's double bass was in the truck when it left Barston. It wasn't in the truck when it got to Barcelona. The truck stopped for a long time only once. And a French driver saw two men with something big and white there. Something like a double bass case.'

'How do you know that?' Adriana asked.

'The French police told us,' the inspector said.

'Where's my double bass now?' I asked.

'I'm sorry, Miss Wade,' said Inspector Portillo.

'But I don't know.' He liked me, I thought. He really was sorry.

'What about the painting?' Martin asked.

'That's safe,' Inspector Portillo said. 'The French police found it this morning in Paris.'

'Excuse me!' Adriana said.

'Yes?' said Inspector Portillo.

'You said Frank died because of the truck. But how? Why? What do you mean? Did he die because of the painting? Did he put the painting in Penny's double bass case, or what?'

'Those are all good questions,' Inspector Portillo replied. 'They were our questions too. At first we didn't understand why Mr Shepherd died. Did he fall out of that window? Did he jump? Did somebody push him? Did he have problems? With a lover? A friend? Was there an argument?'

I looked over at Candida Ashley-Morton. Her head was in her hands. She was crying, I think. Perhaps she really did do it. Inspector Portillo was still speaking.

'But then we talked to the hotel people. We looked at the rooms. And immediately we had a problem.'

'What problem?' Martin asked.

'The window in Mr Shepherd's room was closed,' Inspector Portillo said.

'He didn't like open windows,' Candida said quietly.

'That is correct.' Inspector Portillo looked at Candida when he said this. 'And a man cannot jump out of a closed window.'

'What are you saying?' Martin asked.

'I am saying that Frank Shepherd didn't jump out of the window of his room. He fell from a different room.'

There was silence in the hotel dining room now – complete silence.

'That was difficult for us,' the inspector said. 'Whose room was it? We didn't know. But then one of my men looked at everything on the hotel computer. He looked at the telephone calls. Then he saw it. Somebody telephoned the police in London last night. What was the room number? He looked on the computer. It was Frank Shepherd's room. Frank Shepherd telephoned London.'

'Frank called the police in London?' Marilyn asked. 'Why?'

'We asked the police in London the same question. "Why did Frank Shepherd telephone you?" They told us.'

'Wait a minute,' Martin said. 'I thought Frank fell from somebody else's window. But you said he telephoned from his room.'

'You are quite correct,' the inspector said. 'He telephoned from his room. Then he went to somebody else's room.'

'Whose?' Candida asked. 'Do you know what happened to Frank. Do you know the name of his killer?'

'Oh yes, we know. We know.' And suddenly I knew too.

Chapter 10 *Why did you do it?*

Sometimes, now, I still can't believe what happened in Barcelona. I don't know the whole story, of course, but I know most of it.

Simon did not stay for the second half of the concert in the theatre in Barcelona that night. 'No problem,' he thought, 'Penny saw me at the concert. The orchestra saw me. Penny thinks I'm sitting at the back.' Poor Simon.

Simon went to a bar to meet someone. But Frank was also in the bar. Frank needed a drink. He needed to think about his problems. You see Frank loved Candida. But then Marilyn decided that she loved Frank too. She sent him letters, gave him things, talked to him, followed him everywhere. Frank didn't like Marilyn following him. He needed a drink.

Simon didn't see Frank. Frank didn't see Simon either, at first. But the barman saw Frank – and later he saw a picture of Frank on the television – so he rang the police.

A tall Frenchman came into the bar with a black bag. Perhaps that's when Frank looked up and saw Simon, but he didn't speak to him. Frank knew that something wasn't right.

'Thank you *Monsieur* Hunt,' the Frenchman said. 'We have got the picture. My friend is very happy.' He opened his bag. He gave Simon a large brown envelope. Frank was listening.

'All this, just for a Cézanne painting,' Simon laughed.

41

Frank probably remembered the article in the newspaper. The Frenchman walked out of the bar. Simon looked into the envelope. There was money in it. A lot of money. Frank saw it too. It was money for 'The Gardener' by Cézanne, of course. Frank didn't know the whole story then, but we know now: a rich man in France wanted it for his secret collection of art. Something else Frank didn't know. Simon's cousin worked at the Tate Gallery as a security guard. She took the painting from the gallery. She gave it to Simon and he put it in my double bass case. Nobody looks for a painting in a double bass case in an orchestra truck!

Simon went back to the hotel. Frank went to his own room first and made that phone call to London. Then he went to Simon's room. Perhaps he wanted to ask him, 'Why? Why did you do it?' Perhaps he wanted to tell him to run. I don't know. But it wasn't a good idea to go to Simon's room. Simon's window was open. Frank fell five floors to the ground.

The police found Simon at Barcelona airport. He went there after his night with me.

*   *   *

The policeman walked through the police station. I followed him. It was very hot in the building.

We got to a door. The policeman unlocked the door.

There was a different policeman in the room. And Simon.

'Hello,' Simon said. He looked terrible.

'Hello,' I said quietly. 'How are you?'

'What do you think?' he said. It wasn't a real question.

'Oh Simon, did you really kill Frank?' I asked him.

42

'Yes. No. He was angry. He fell. Well, I pushed him.'

'Why?' I asked. I couldn't believe this.

'He saw me in the bar,' Simon said in an unfriendly voice. 'He saw me with the Frenchman. He knew about "The Gardener".'

'Why?' I shouted. 'Why did you do it?' I was very angry.

'Why did I do it? Money, of course. I wanted more money.'

'And why didn't you run?' I asked.

'I did. After Frank "fell", I left the hotel. But then I

thought. "Nobody knows. It was an accident. That's what people will say." But I didn't know about his telephone call. I didn't know that the police could see where his fingers were, his fingerprints on the window of my room.'

We sat in that room for a few more minutes. We didn't look at each other.

'What's going to happen to you?' I asked.

'What do you think? I'm going to be in prison for a long time, I expect.'

'Poor Simon.'

'Oh, be quiet. Go away. Go away. I don't want you in this room. I don't want anybody here with me. I don't want to see you again. Ever. Just get out.'

I wanted to stay. Simon was not a good person, but I loved him. Well, I loved him once upon a time.

'Simon,' I said. 'Simon I . . .' but I didn't have any words in my head. Simon looked at the floor. The Spanish policeman looked out of the window. I left the room.

When I walked out of the police station I didn't look back.

Chapter 11   *One more question*

We left Barcelona. I was very unhappy. I thought about Simon in prison. We played concerts in Madrid and Bilbao. We didn't play very well, of course, but we played.

On our last night in Bilbao, Adriana and I went out after the concert.

'Are you going to be all right?' Adriana said. 'You've had a terrible time.'

We were walking by the Río Nervión, Bilbao's big, black river.

'Adriana,' I said. 'Can I ask you something?'

'Yes, of course.'

'Do you – did you like Simon before?'

'Well, I liked him.'

'Were you very good friends?'

'What? What are you asking? Like lovers?' Adriana asked.

'No. Yes. No. I don't know.' Why did I start this, I thought.

'Of course he wasn't my lover,' she laughed. 'Why did you think that?'

'I didn't, really. It's just, well, you had a secret.'

'Ah. That . . . ' She stopped and looked at me.

'You did have a secret, didn't you?' I asked.

'Yes, yes we did.' She was silent for a minute. I waited. 'Simon saw us, you see. He saw me with Martin.'

'Martin!' Now I was really surprised.

'Yes. We've been together for three months. But we didn't want to tell anyone.'

'So the night Simon killed Frank?' I asked. 'Somebody was in your room . . .'

'You thought it was Simon! Oh, Penny!'

'I'm sorry,' I said.

'It was Martin, of course, you silly thing.' She laughed.

'I'm sorry,' I said again.

'Now listen to me,' said Adriana. 'Don't feel sorry, don't think about Simon. Start your life again. Start thinking of the future.'

That's when I heard it. Music. Someone was playing a guitar. Somebody else was playing a violin. But that wasn't all. There was another instrument too.

'Adriana!' I shouted. 'Listen!'

'What?'

'That sound. I know that sound. Come on.'

We ran by the side of the river. We ran to the music. The players in the street were very good. We stood there, listening to the guitar and the violin. And a double bass. A beautiful double bass with a special sound. A Panormo. Made in 1798. It was my double bass.

'Hey,' I said. 'That's my double bass.'

'No, it isn't,' said the double bass player.

'All right,' I said, 'Where did you get it?'

'Well, I . . . er . . . I . . . it's mine,' he said again.

'That's not true,' Adriana said. 'It's not your double bass and you know it!'

The double bass player was not sure what to do. He didn't look very happy. He knew that something was wrong.

'All right,' he said. 'All right. A man sold it to me. Very cheap. In the street. It wasn't right. I know. But I don't like it anyway. The sound is all wrong. You give me some money and you can have it.'

Finally we gave him some money, but not much. I went to the bass player and took the lovely instrument. It was dirty and there were some black lines on the wood. But I loved it anyway. I was very happy. I put my arms around it.

'Come on,' I said to it. 'Let's go home.'

At that moment a car came round the corner and stopped. Two policemen got out. I didn't know the first one, but I knew the second.

'Ah,' he said. 'Hello Miss Wade. Penny.'

'Inspector Portillo,' I said. 'What are you doing here? You work in Barcelona.'

'That is true. I work in Barcelona.'

'So why are you here?'

'We ask the questions,' he said. He was laughing at me. 'You have found something, I see,' he said.

'Yes, it's my double bass. Isn't it fantastic!'

'It is good news, yes. You said it was a very good double bass. It looks nice. But I think its player is more beautiful.'

'Sorry?' I said.

'Why do you think I am in Bilbao, Penny Wade?' the inspector said. He *was* very good-looking.

'Come on, Penny,' Adriana said. 'It's time we went back to the hotel.'

'I will take you,' my inspector said. 'Your double bass can go in our car, I think. Come on. Then I want to ask Miss Wade a question.'

'More questions! I don't believe it.' I said.

'Only one,' he said. 'I've only got one more question.'

And he did ask me one more question. The most surprising question in the world. And my answer? 'I'll think about it.' And I have thought about it. Maybe there is a future after all. I'm going back to Spain tomorrow.